FUTURE READY
LIBRARY AND **MEDIA**
CENTER MASTERY

LYRIC GREEN AND ANN GRAHAM GAINES

Enslow Publishing
101 W. 23rd Street
Suite 240
New York, NY 10011
USA

enslow.com

Published in 2018 by Enslow Publishing, LLC
101 W. 23rd Street, Suite 240, New York, NY 10011

Library of Congress Cataloging-in-Publication Data

Names: Green, Lyric, author. | Gaines, Ann Graham, author.
Title: Future ready library and media center mastery / Lyric Green and Ann Graham Gaines.
Description: New York : Enslow Publishing, 2018. | Series: Future ready project skills | Includes bibliographical references and index. |
Audience: Grade 3 to 6.
Identifiers: LCCN 2017001295| ISBN 9780766086579 (library-bound) | ISBN 9780766087774 (pbk.) | ISBN 9780766087781 (6-pack)
Subjects: LCSH: Libraries--Juvenile literature. | Instructional materials centers--Juvenile literature. | Library research--Juvenile literature. | Information resources--Juvenile literature.
Classification: LCC Z665.5 .G738 2018 | DDC 027--dc23
LC record available at https://lccn.loc.gov/2017001295

Printed in China

To Our Readers: We have done our best to make sure all website addresses in this book were active and appropriate when we went to press. However, the author and the publisher have no control over and assume no liability for the material available on those websites or on any websites they may link to. Any comments or suggestions can be sent by email to customerservice@ enslow.com.

Portions of this book originally appeared in the book *Ace it! Master the Library and Media Center Skills*.

Photo Credits: Cover, pp. 1, 4, 10, 19, 28, 38 Photosani/Shutterstock.com; p. 3 David Arts/Shutterstock.com; p. 5 Corbis/ VCG/Getty Images; p. 6 William Manning/Corbis/Getty Images; pp. 6 (background), 14, 15, 23, 33, 36, 40 vvlinkov/Shutterstock.com (adapted); p. 7 Comstock Images/Stockbyte/Thinkstock; p. 8 Nukul Chanada/Shutterstock.com; p. 11 asiseeit/E+/ Getty Images; p. 13 Stuart Boulton/Alamy Stock Photo; p. 16 Jupiterimages/Stockbyte/Thinkstock; p. 20 JGI/Tom Grill/Blend Images/Getty Images; p. 22 Russell Burden/Photolibrary/Getty Images; p. 25 moodboard/Thinkstock29 Wuka/E+/Getty Images; p. 30 Roy Morsch/Corbis/Getty Images; p. 32 Wendy Stone/Corbis/Getty Images; p. 34 Montgomery Martin/Alamy Stock Photo; p. 39 Tetra Images/Alamy Stock Photo.

CONTENTS

CHAPTER 1

AT THE LIBRARY!

The library is a wonderful place. A lot of people go to the library. Many of them are kids like you. What are they doing there? People go to the library for many different reasons. At the library you can pick out a book to read, flip through the latest magazines, check out a new DVD, or listen to music.

The library is a good place to do research. When you do research, you search for information about something that interests you. You search through sources, like books, magazines, and newspapers, to find information and to answer your questions.

Kids often do research for school assignments. You might also do research as part of an after-school activity. For example, you might enter a science fair, or maybe you want to earn a scout badge. Then you will have to hunt for specific

You can find almost anything at the library!

MORE THAN ONE KIND OF LIBRARY

Public libraries are the type of library that most people use. If your town is large, it might have more than one public library. Many big cities have one main library, with smaller branch libraries in different parts of town. If you go to a branch library, you can request materials from all the other libraries in your town.

Colleges and universities also have libraries. You probably won't be able to check out materials, but you can usually go inside and use their resources.

Another kind of library is the special collection. These libraries contain rare items that can't be found anywhere else. Special collections can include old books, maps, letters, legal documents, music, photographs, and pieces of art.

The Library of Congress is the most famous special collection in the United States. This library was founded in 1800. It has more than 134 million different items and more than 500 miles of bookshelves! The Library of Congress owns the first book printed in the United States. It also holds one of the first movies ever made, early baseball cards, and a photograph of Abraham Lincoln when he became president. You can visit the Library of Congress in Washington, DC.

A librarian can help you find what you need in the library. They're experts at research!

information to learn about your topic. A third reason to do research is for yourself. Research is the perfect way to learn more about a hobby or interest. You might want to know more about soccer, comic books, or a favorite TV show.

You can do research in many different places. Lots of people like to find information right at home. They use their own

Don't write in library books! Be sure to keep a notebook with you, so you can take notes.

books or a computer or tablet with internet access. The best place to do research, though, is at a library.

Many people think of libraries as places to go to get books. But libraries are much more! Today's libraries are entire media centers. They have magazines, newspapers, DVDs, CDs, and, of course, books. People go to libraries to use the internet. Visitors also use the library's digital sources, such as databases with thousands of magazine articles. You can get all the information you need at a library!

On top of that, libraries have one great resource that you won't find anywhere else—the librarian, or media specialist.

Librarians are specially trained to help people use the library. Think of librarians as detectives. They will use clues to hunt for information you need. They'll also help you learn to find the information on your own. You'll use this skill for your whole life.

CHAPTER 2

MUCH MORE THAN BOOKS

First things first: get to know your library! Most libraries have a website. If you have a computer at home, ask your parents to help you look for the site. You can also ask your school librarian or teacher to show you. Simply type the name of your town and "public library" into the search field of your favorite search engine.

THE LIBRARY ON THE WEB

If your public library has a website, you should see it right at the top of your results list in your search engine. Click on the link and take a look. You'll see something like the site on the next page. You will find basic information, such as the library's address and phone number, when it's open, and how to get a library card. Getting a library card is easy, usually free, and available for anyone.

When you check out a book from the library, be sure you remember when you have to return it.

Many library websites let you search the library catalog. This is a huge database of all the items available in the library. A database is a large collection of information. Some websites even have a map or floor plan, so you can see how your library is organized.

Library websites also tell you about their services. The library has computers for the public to use. Many libraries also have programs and special events for kids and other members of the community. For example, a famous author might give a reading of their latest book. Librarians often host a kids' book club. Some even show movies or have game nights.

GETTING TO KNOW YOUR LIBRARY

Once you get to the library, take a tour. You can look around by yourself, but the best way is to have a librarian give you a guided tour. Some libraries have helpful handouts and maps. Ask any librarian for help.

A tour might start at the library's circulation desk. This is where you go to check out books and other materials. Your next stop will probably be the library catalog. The catalog is on a computer or many computers, depending on the size of the library.

Most libraries have three main rooms or areas. One is especially for adults. The second is for children. The third area is the reference collection. The books in a reference collection are filled with easy-to-find facts. Encyclopedias and dictionaries are two types of reference books. Other kinds are atlases—books filled with maps—and town records. Library visitors use reference books so often that librarians want to keep them in the building. These books do not circulate. This means people cannot check them out and take them home. But you can read them in the library and photocopy the parts you need.

The call numbers on library books help you know where to find them and help keep the library organized.

To help find a book at the library, find out this information:

TYPE OF SOURCE: book, audiobook, DVD, magazine, newspaper
NAME OF AUTHOR:
TITLE:
CALL NUMBER:

Once you know what you're looking for, figure out where to find it in the library

NONFICTION
FICTION
CHILDREN'S SECTION
MAGAZINE SECTION
AUDIO COLLECTION
REFERENCE
OVERSIZE

MORE THAN ONE KIND OF LIBRARIAN

Big libraries have different kinds of librarians. The reference librarian's job is to help people do their research. This person sits at a special reference desk. He or she can show you how to use the library's reference materials. The reference librarian will also help you find books, magazines, and articles on a computer. You'll get lots of creative ideas for your research project.

Libraries keep fiction and nonfiction in separate sections. Fiction books are about made-up topics, and nonfiction books are about the real world. Fiction is usually arranged by authors' last names. Nonfiction books are what you mostly use for research. They are arranged by subject. For example, books about baseball are near other books about baseball— and also near books about other sports, like football and volleyball. Many libraries have a special nonfiction section for biographies—books about real-life people.

Librarians know about more than books! They can also help you search the internet for information.

HOW TO FIND A BOOK

Librarians use a classification system to arrange books called the Dewey decimal system. Every book gets its own call number. This is a series of numbers followed by letters or more numbers. The call number is printed on a sticker and taped on the spine of the book. On the shelf, books are arranged in order by call number. You can find out a book's call number in the library catalog. Libraries also buy magazines and newspapers. They are usually kept on shelves in a special periodicals area. A periodical is a publication that comes out every so often—for example, once a week or once a month.

Most libraries have CDs, DVDs, and educational video games for visitors to check out. These materials have their own special areas, too.

Your librarian can show you where to find computers. Library computers have many different purposes. Some are just for librarians to use. Others hold the catalog or other databases about specific topics. On other computers, visitors can sign up to use the internet.

SEARCHING ON YOUR OWN

Once you're familiar with the library, you're ready to start your hunt for information. First, learn to use your library's catalog. Catalogs let you search in different ways. If you are looking for a specific book, you can do a title search. This means you type in the book's title. If you are looking for books by a certain author, you can do an author search. This means you type in the author's name.

You can also do a catalog search by subject or keyword. Let's say you want to learn about sharks. If you enter the word shark into the subject box and press ENTER, the screen will show a list of sources. For each source, you'll see the title, author, and call number. Click on a source to see more information about it. Then you will find out when, where, and by what company the source was published. You will need this information for when you create a bibliography, or a list of the sources you used in your research.

Let's say you want to go and find a book on the shelf. First, write down the title and call number. In the next chapter, you'll find out how to search for magazine and newspaper articles.

CHAPTER 3

MAPPING OUT YOUR RESEARCH

L et's say your teacher has assigned you a research project. Your project will turn out better if you create a plan for your assignment first. You'll save time and stay focused on your goals.

To make sure your paper will get finished in time, make a schedule. Figure out how long you have to do your assignment. Then give yourself due dates for each step. Experts say you should plan to spend about 35 percent of your time researching. You'll spend most of that time at the library. For the rest of your time, you will write and finish your project.

Take the time to review your assignment. What, exactly, is it that you are researching? What is the goal of your research? Even if you're doing research for fun, you should think about your goal. Write down what you already know about your topic. Next, make a list of the questions you want to answer.

Taking notes while reading can help you keep track of all the information you've found on your topic.

Let's say you're working on a poster about volcanoes. Here are some examples of research questions: Why do volcanoes erupt? Where do volcanoes form? How often do they erupt? Now you can narrow your research topic even more. Perhaps you decide to create a map of the most active volcanoes in the world.

KEYWORDS ARE KEY

After you come up with questions, it's time to brainstorm for keywords. These are the words you use to search in the library catalog. Keywords can be tricky, because you don't want them to be too general or too specific. For example, if you want to know about volcanoes, the keyword *mountains* will give you too much information. A lot of sources about mountains won't tell you anything about volcanoes! On the other hand, if you use the words *Mt. Vesuvius*, you'll only find information about that one volcano. That search is too narrow.

Your keywords should be somewhere in the middle. For a report about Pluto, two good keywords might be *Pluto facts*. It also helps to write down synonyms for your keywords. That way you'll have lots of words to try. If one set of keywords doesn't work, you may be able to find the right information using a different set of words.

Now, think about the kind of information you are hoping to find. For a school assignment, you might have to include lots of facts. For a biography, you might need to find a person's diary or letters. Are you required to put quotations from

Giving a presentation doesn't have to be scary. If you're well prepared and have researched your topic well, your presentation will be easier than you thought!

CREATING A RESEARCH PLAN

Creating a research plan can be very helpful when you're doing a project. Think about what it is you need to know, and what other information might be useful.

What I want to find out
My main question
Other questions:
Keywords
Sources I'd like to find
Illustrations

experts in your research project? Make a checklist of requirements for your assignment, or use the rubric that your teacher gave you. A rubric is a list of everything your teacher wants you to do for your research project.

Your project might require you to use photographs or illustrations. Pictures can show some things better than words can. For example, it's hard to describe the location of a shark's nostrils, but a picture or diagram does the job easily. You might also decide to look for maps, charts, or graphs. These visual elements make your project more complete and exciting for your audience.

SPIDER MAP

This is a spider map. The research topic is inside the center circle. In the outside circles, there are keywords to use in a hunt for information.

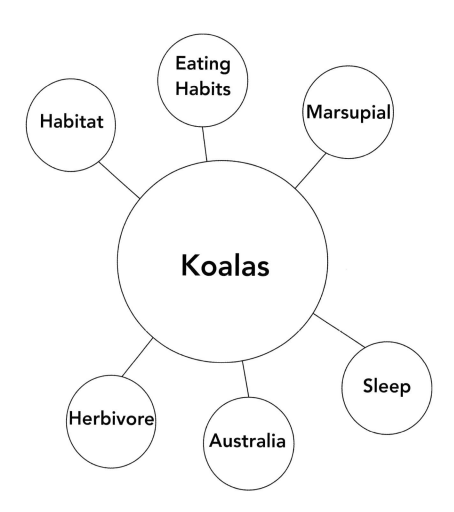

The library is a great place to find lots of sources for your research project.

SOURCES, SOURCES, SOURCES

Next, think about what kinds of sources you need. Many teachers require you to use more than one kind of source for a research project. Books and magazines are great sources, but don't stop there. The internet is a very popular source because it contains so much up-to-date information. You can find millions of pages full of information without ever leaving your chair! Just remember that not all information is helpful information. Be mindful of the sites you visit.

Many organizations, such as the National Geographic Society and PBS, make excellent documentary movies about history or science. Your library probably has a wide selection of these educational films. Audio material, such as a recording of an expert giving a lecture, can be another great source.

MORE THAN ONE LIBRARY IN TOWN

Keep in mind that you can go beyond your own town's library. Let's say your library does not have a DVD about ballet dancers. You can ask the librarian to borrow one through an interlibrary loan. That means your library will borrow the DVD from another library and then you can borrow it from your library.

The American Library Association (ALA) says that people in today's world must become "information smart." What does this mean? It's important for us all—students, teachers, parents, and others—to know "how to find, evaluate

and use the best, most current information available to us."
We need to know when to use books, when to search on the
internet, and when to find another source. We live in a world
full of information. The difficult part can be finding the right
information.

CHAPTER 4

MAKING THE MOST OF YOUR SOURCES

I t's now time to begin your research. A good place to start is by finding basic information in a reference book, such as an encyclopedia. Then you can start your library catalog search. Maybe you already know about a great book on your topic. You have the name of the book or the author. Then you can do a title or author search. If you don't have a book in mind, start your catalog search with keywords you have picked out.

DIVING INTO RESEARCH

After entering in your keywords, you will get a list of titles. When you get the results list, you will probably see that some titles will not help you. That might be because they are fiction books. Or perhaps they are about history, but you are only interested in information from this year. Pick out the sources that do look helpful. Write down their call numbers, and then find them on the shelves. If a promising source is already checked out, ask a librarian to put the title on hold. When the source gets returned, the library will give you a call.

Go through your new sources one by one. Your mission is to decide which books will help you answer your research questions. Use a book's table of contents to find out the titles of its chapters. Go to the very back of the book to find the index. An index is an alphabetical list of the subjects in the book. (Turn to page 47 to see what an index looks like). Look for your research keywords in the index, and then turn to the pages listed.

The library card catalog will help you find the books you need.

Once you have selected your materials for research, read through them to see which sources will be helpful.

Quickly skim through the book. Look for good illustrations, charts, or maps. If you decide a book will not be useful, put it aside right away. Don't waste your time, move on. Another book will have the information you need.

OTHER SOURCES

If you have found DVDs about your topic, look at their cases and read the descriptions. If you want to watch a movie, your library might have a place where you can view it there. Otherwise, you'll have to check it out to watch it at home.

The card catalog won't help you find some of the greatest sources—magazines and newspapers. Ask a librarian to show you how to use periodical indexes and databases. These sources often have more up-to-date information than books, and can be a great resource for your project!

You might find more sources than you can use right away. On the other hand, maybe you won't find enough. Maybe you used too many keywords, or your keywords were too specific. To find more sources, browse the library bookshelves. Go back to the area where you found one useful book, and look for others. You can also switch your keywords and do your search again. Now is the best time to get help from a librarian.

Look inside your best sources to find more information. Did you know that nonfiction books usually have a bibliography at the end? Use the bibliography like a miniature catalog. You might find some of these sources right in your own library!

Libraries have more than just books! They also have media centers where you can use computers to search the internet.

Here's an example of how to organize your notes as you do research.

MY RESEARCH TOPIC: SHARKS

My Question:
The Answer:
Where I Found It (Name of Source):

My Second Question:
The Answer:
Where I Found It (Name of Source):

You can have as many questions and answers as you'd like. The more answers, the better your project will be!

What do you do once you've found good sources? Use them! As you read, take good notes. Notes will keep your facts straight as you create your paper, presentation, mural, or another project.

CHECKING OUT YOUR SOURCES

You might want to take your best sources home. Then you can keep using them. First, you will have to get a library card. Your family might already have a card. If not, you will have to apply for one. The librarian will ask you to fill out a form with your name, address, and phone number. Some libraries may

Once you have a library card, you can check out books any time you want.

need a parent or guardian signature. You might also have to pay a small fee. Then you will receive your library card.

To check out materials, go to the circulation desk. Hand the librarian the materials and your library card.

Most libraries use a computer to scan your card and a label on the book. This records what you've checked out. Then the librarian will tell you when your materials are due back. You will probably be able to keep books for about two weeks. Your library might have a limit on how many items you can check out. Then you'll have to make a few different trips.

Be sure to follow your library's borrowing rules. First, always return your materials on time. Other people may be waiting to use your sources. Besides, if you don't meet your due date, you will have to pay a fine. If you need more time with a source, you can usually renew it. Another rule is to take good care of the materials you check out. Don't let anything become damaged! You will have to pay for a new copy.

Remember that some library sources cannot be checked out. If you need information from reference books or magazines, you have two choices. You can either take notes at the library or make a photocopy of the pages you need.

ONLINE SAFETY

The internet is a great source for information. But it can also be a very dangerous place. Many websites are not appropriate for kids. Some websites may ask for personal information,

DON'T STEAL PEOPLE'S WORDS!

Plagiarism is a serious mistake. When you plagiarize, you steal another person's work, such as words or pictures. Then you pretend the work is yours. You can avoid this by taking careful notes. Never write down exact sentences unless you are planning to use them as a quotation. When you do quote someone's words, make sure to place quotation marks ("") around them. Be sure to tell your readers the name of the person who did the work you are using. Include the source in your bibliography.

Teachers think plagiarism is a very serious problem. If they think you plagiarized by mistake, they might let you rewrite the paper. If your teacher thinks you should have known the rules, you could be in big trouble.

such as your name, age, address, photograph, or telephone number. Never give out any information—always ask a trusted adult like a teacher, parent, or guardian for help.

To stay safe when you're on the internet, get away from sites that make you feel uncomfortable. Never give out personal information or send your photograph to a website without asking a trusted adult first. Most important, never make arrangements to go and see someone you have met on the internet.

CHAPTER 5

THE RIGHT SOURCES

There are so many interesting sources in libraries, how will you choose which ones to use for your research? You are going to evaluate them. This means you make sure that the sources have correct, helpful information. How can you do this?

FINDING THE NEWEST SOURCES

First, check how old the source is. It's usually a good idea to look for the most up-to-date information. In the subject of science, for example, we discover new information every day. Even sources from two years ago could be wrong!

Next, check out the author. After you find a name, find out who the person is. In a good source, the author is an expert. Look for an author who has studied their subject for many years.

If you've done your research, you'll find your project much easier than you imagined.

EVALUATING A WEBSITE

Use a checklist like this one to evaluate the websites you visit. It will help you decide whether the source is accurate and helpful.

What is the address of the website?

Is the spelling correct?

Are the author's name and email address on the page? (This could be a person or an organization.)

Are the links easy to find?

Are the words easy to read?

Is there a date that tells you when the page was made?

Do the photographs looks real and professional?

Do the photographs on the site help you learn about the topic?

Does the site tell you who took the photographs?

Does the title tell you what the site is about?

Does the site answer some of your research questions?

Does the author of the page say things that you know are wrong?

Does the author include a bibliography?

WEBSITES HAVE AUTHORS, TOO!

If you're looking at a website, you want to know who created it. It could be an organization—like a college or a museum—instead of a person. To find the author of a website, look at the bottom of the page. If you don't find any author information, ask a librarian or teacher for help.

Also notice if the author mentions the sources that he or she used. You should stay away from books, articles, and websites that don't tell where they got their information. Always use sources that give you the chance to check what they say. It's a good idea to double check some facts to see if they are accurate. On one site, you might see that a venus fly trap can eat a spider every ten days. But another source might tell you they need to eat ten flies every day. Check a few more sources to make sure you get the real facts.

Last, make sure that the source is relevant to what you are writing. This means that it is closely related to your topic. An article on supernovas might be interesting, but if you are researching the Milky Way galaxy, it probably won't help you.

Soon, you'll become comfortable using a library to do research. You'll be a pro on its wide variety of resources, and learn how to work well with a librarian. Your library skills will help you all through school, in college, and as an adult.

GLOSSARY

bibliography A list of sources used to write a paper, article, or book.

brainstorm To come up with ideas and write them down as they pop into your head.

call number An assigned number that says where a library book should go on the shelves.

catalog A computer database or collection of cards that lists all the sources that a library holds.

circulate To move to and from a library, like a book when someone borrows and then returns it.

circulation desk The desk where you check out library materials.

databases Collections of information kept on a computer.

Dewey decimal system A system for organizing nonfiction books. Every book has a number that tells where it should go on a library shelf.

diagram A plan or drawing that shows all the parts of something, such as a frog's body or a snowmobile.

evaluate To decide if something is good or bad.

index A list at the back of a book that tells you all the things you can read about in the book.

interlibrary loan When libraries borrow materials from each other.

keyword A word that a researcher uses to search for a topic in a catalog, database, or internet search engine.

media All the different forms that information can come in, including books, magazines, the internet, radio programs, CDs, and DVDs.

plagiarism Stealing someone else's work and pretending it is your own.

quotations The exact words that a person spoke or wrote.

reference collection A group of nonfiction materials including encyclopedias, atlases, and other sources of facts. These materials cannot be checked out of a library.

reference librarian A librarian who helps people find information in reference sources.

relevant Closely related to a certain topic.

renew To extend the due date for a library item.

research A hunt for information about a particular topic.

resource A source of help or information.

rubric A list of requirements for an assignment.

services Ways to help customers or visitors. For example, a library provides the service of lending books.

skim To look through a piece of writing quickly, without reading every word.

sources Publications that supply information, such as books, articles, videos, and recordings.

FURTHER READING

BOOKS

Graham, Leland, and Isabelle McCoy. *How to Write a Great Research Paper*. Chicago, IL: Incentive Publications by World Book, 2014.

Greenberg, Michael. *Painless Study Techniques*. Hauppauge, NY: Barron's Educational Publishing, 2016.

Jakubiak, David J. *A Smart Kid's Guide to Doing Internet Research*. New York, NY: Powerkids Press, 2009.

Strausser, Jefferey. *Painless Writing (3rd Edition)*. Hauppauge, NY: Barron's Educational Publishing, 2016.

WEBSITES

Great Websites for Kids

gws.ala.org

A list of recommended kids' sites for research on many topics.

Kids.gov

kids.usa.gov

A government-run website that covers many topics including science, history, art, music, and more!

National Geographic Kids

kids.nationalgeographic.com

A great place to start internet research about animals and science.

INDEX